READING RAINBOW LIBRARY

The Banza

CONTENTS

This book is a presentation of Weekly Reader Books. Weekly Reader Books offers book clubs for children from preschool through high school.

For further information write to:
Weekly Reader Books
4343 Equity Drive
Columbus, Ohio 43228

Weekly Reader Books offers several exciting card and activity programs. For information, write to WEEKLY READER BOOKS, P.O. Box 16636, Columbus, Ohio 43216.

The Banza adapted for this volume by arrangement with Dial Books for Young Readers, a Division of E.P. Dutton, a Division of New American Library.

This **Reading Rainbow Library** volume designed by Marsha Cohen/Parallelogram.

"Behind the Scenes" and "Activities" sections: Mary Ann Gray, writer; Kris Nielsen, illustrator.

Reading Rainbow Library created and produced by Reading Rainbow Gazette, Inc., 1501 Third Avenue, New York, New York 10028.

The Banza

A Haitian story by
DIANE WOLKSTEIN

Pictures by
MARC BROWN

The Dial Press
New York

10419
398
WOL

Dial Books for Young Readers
A Division of E. P. Dutton, Inc.
2 Park Avenue
New York, New York 10016

For Mme. Gurewich,
who teaches the big and small song
and always the song of the heart
D. W.

To Nancy Bryan,
who saved me from becoming
a brain surgeon
M. B.

On the island of Haiti there once lived a little tiger named Teegra and a little goat named Cabree. Usually tigers and goats are enemies, but these two were best friends.

They had met during a thunderstorm when they had each run into the same cave for shelter. The storm had lasted all night, and when they came out in the morning, everything seemed strange to them, for they had come out of the cave by a different entrance and were lost.

They were both quite small, lonely, and afraid.

They looked at each other.

Cabree brayed, "Be-be...."

Teegra roared, "Rrr...."

"Do you want to be friends?" Cabree asked.

"Now!" Teegra answered.

So they wandered over the countryside, playing together, sharing whatever food they found, and sleeping close to each other at night for warmth.

Then one morning they found themselves in front of the cave where they had first met.

"rrRRRRR!"

Cabree turned. But it was not Teegra who had roared.

"RRRRRRrrr-rrRR!"

It was a roar of another tiger.

"Mama! Papa! *Auntie!*" Teegra cried joyfully as three huge tigers bounded out of the bushes.

Cabree ran into the cave without waiting.

After a while Teegra went to find Cabree, but Cabree refused to come out of the cave, so Teegra went home with his family.

The next morning Teegra went to the cave alone.

"Cabree!" he called. "I brought you a banza."

Cabree poked her head out of the cave.

"A *ban-za*? What's that?"

"A little banjo," Teegra said. "It belonged to my uncle, but I want you to have it—so it will protect you."

"How will the banza protect me?" Cabree asked.

"Auntie says, 'The banza belongs to the heart, and there is no stronger protection than the heart.' When you play the banza, Auntie says to place it over your heart, and 'one day the heart and banza will be one.'"

"Is that true?"

"Oh, Cabree, I don't really know, but I know I shall not forget you."

Teegra placed the banza around his friend's neck, then he turned to go.

"Where are you going?" Cabree asked.

"Home!" Teegra answered, and the little tiger ran back to his family without stopping.

Cabree stepped out of the cave so she could see the banza more clearly. It was a beautiful banza, and when the sun shone on it, it gleamed. Cabree held the banza over her heart. She stroked it gently. A friendly, happy sound came out. She stroked it again—and again—and before she realized it, she was trotting through the forest, humming to herself and stopping now and then to play a tune on the banza.

One afternoon Cabree came to a spring. She wanted
to drink, but she was afraid the banza would get wet, so
she took it off and carefully laid it down in the bushes.
As she drank the cool sweet water she heard a low
growl behind her.

"rrrRRrrr...."

Turning quickly, Cabree saw four large hungry tigers.
Cabree wanted to leap across the stream and run away,
but the banza was in the bushes behind the tigers. No!
She would not leave the banza Teegra had given her.

Slowly and fiercely Cabree walked toward the banza.

Another tiger appeared. Now there were five.

Cabree kept walking.

"Where are you going?" the leader shouted.

Cabree reached the bushes. She picked up the banza and hung it around her neck. Then she turned to the tigers. Five more jumped out of the bushes.

Now there were ten!

"What have you put around your neck?" asked the leader.

And Cabree, trying to quiet her thundering, pounding heart, brought her foreleg to her chest and, by mistake, plucked the banza.

"A musician!" said the chief, laughing. "So you wish to play us a song?"

"No!" said Cabree.

"No?" echoed the leader. And all the tigers took a step closer to Cabree.

Teegra! Cabree wanted to shout. But Teegra was far away, and she was alone, surrounded by the tigers. No, she was not completely alone. She still had the banza Teegra had given her.

Cabree's heart beat very fast, but in time to her heartbeat she stroked the banza. She opened her mouth, and a song came out. To her own surprise it was a loud, low, ferocious song:

> *Ten fat tigers, ten fat tigers,*
> *Cabree eats tigers raw.*
> *Yesterday Cabree ate ten tigers;*
> *Today Cabree eats ten more.*

The tigers were astonished.

"Who is Cabree? And where did you learn that song?" demanded the chief.

"I am Cabree." Cabree answered in a new deep voice, and noticing how frightened the tigers looked, she added, "And that is *my* song. I always sing it before dinner."

The tiger chief realized that three of his tigers had suddenly disappeared.

"Madame Cabree," he said, "you play beautifully. Permit me to offer you a drink."

"Very well," said Cabree.

"Bring Madame Cabree a drink!" he ordered the two tigers closest to him, and as they started to leave he whispered, "and don't come back."

Five tigers stared at Madame Cabree.

Cabree stared back. Then she stroked her banza and sang, a little slower, but just as intently:

Five fat tigers, five fat tigers,
Cabree eats tigers raw.
Yesterday Cabree ate ten tigers;
Today Cabree eats five more.

"Oh! Oh-h-h! Something dreadful must have happened to my tigers," said the leader. "You." He motioned to the two tigers nearest him. "Go fetch Madame Cabree a drink." And again he whispered, "And don't come back."

Now only three tigers quaked before Madame
Cabree. Cabree sang again:

> *Three fat tigers, three fat tigers,*
> *Cabree eats tigers raw.*
> *Yesterday Cabree ate ten tigers;*
> *Today Cabree eats three more.*

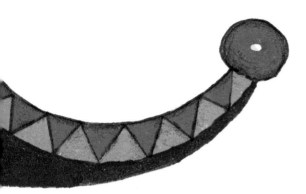

When she finished her song, only the leader re-mained. Cabree began:

One fat tiger—

"Please," whispered the leader, "please let me go. I promise no tiger will ever bother you again."

Cabree looked at the trembling tiger. All she had done was to play the banza and sing what was in her heart. So Teegra's Auntie was right. Her heart had protected her. Her heart and her banza.

"Please!" begged the leader. "I'll do whatever you wish."

"Then go at once to Teegra, the little tiger who lives near the cave. Tell Teegra: 'Today Cabree's heart and the banza are one.'"

"Yes, yes," said the tiger. "'Today Cabree's heart and the banza are one.'" And the tiger chief ran off to find Teegra.

With her banza gleaming around her neck, Cabree went trotting through the forest. But every now and then she would stop. She would stroke her banza and sing, for her heart would have a new song.

The End

Author's Note

Sitting on a stone wall outside the home of Mme. Bellande in Diquini, Haiti, Antoine Exavier told stories one evening in 1973 to Mme. Bellande; my daughter, Rachel; and myself. He began each story by shouting out the word "CRIC?" and we, eager to hear each story, shouted back each time "CRAC!" Antoine called this story "Teegra—Cabree" (pronounced *TEE-gra* and *CAH-bree*), which means "tiger" and "goat" in Creole.

The story stayed with me because of the little goat's silly song, the love shared between the tiger and the goat, and the strange yet beautiful sounding name of an instrument called the *banza*. When I questioned Haitians about the banza, no one seemed to know any more about it than that it was an "old instrument." (Indeed, Dena J. Epstein, in the series *Music in American Life*, cites documents proving that the banjo originated in Africa and was played in Haiti in the eighteenth century as a hollowed-out calabash with hemp strings called a banza.) That Teegra receives the banza from his uncle also implies it belongs to the heritage, for religious tradition (Voodoo) in Haiti is usually passed by the uncles rather than the fathers. When Cabree makes the banza sing, not only is she expressing her own feelings and humor, but she is also continuing the tradition as well as joining herself to the one from whom she is separated. The ageless themes of love, community, and self-expression are interwoven into this friendly, lively, and often very funny Haitian folktale.

I hope that whoever tells *The Banza* will call out "CRIC?" and those who are listening will call back "CRAC!"

D.W.

Artist's Note

In the illustrations for *The Banza* I have incorporated the elements basic to Haitian art—bright colors, flat shapes, varied patterns—as well as many of the symbols that pervade that art: the palm trees that symbolize joy and liberty, the flowers that signify precious freedoms, even certain Voodoo symbols. The exotic animals that appear in *The Banza* are also found throughout the art of this Caribbean island, reflecting its African and European heritage.

Most of all I have tried to convey the spirit of Haitian art, which is alive with personal, spontaneous feeling, innocent rather than primitive, and always reflective of the artist's own experience.

M.B.

Behind the Scenes

Introduction

Music can sound happy. It can sound sad. Pick a feeling and you can find music that sounds like that feeling. What kind of music was in *The Banza?*

Let's Talk Music

The feelings in music depend not only on the notes used in the music, but also on the instruments playing the notes. Instruments have personalities too. Can you imagine an unhappy banjo, for instance? And certain instruments go well together and some don't. Did you ever notice that there's no bongo drum in an orchestra?

Musical groups—orchestra, rock band, jazz quartet—are made up of the instruments that suit the sound they want to make. Some instruments can express many different feelings, so they can play in more than one kind of musical group.

If you play a violin, you could join an orchestra or a string quartet or even a rock band. In a rock band, a violin might be called a fiddle, another word for the same instrument.

A xylophone is perfect for a dance band. It seems to fit little else though.

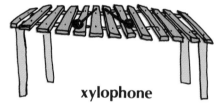

flute

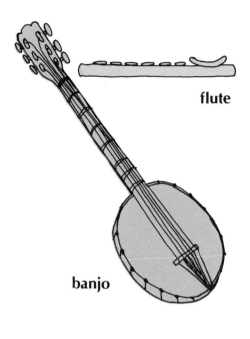

banjo

xylophone

violin

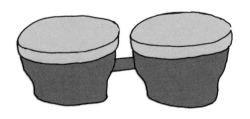

bongo drums

Musical groups play different kinds of music. Orchestras make serious music. It touches the deepest feelings of joy and sadness. A salsa band, on the other hand, makes light, happy music. It makes you want to dance in the sun at a seashore. Rock bands make you want to leap and shout and smile at your friends. Dance bands are made to keep you moving. No one can stand still anywhere near a good dance band.

Think of musical instruments you know—tuba, guitar, kettle drum, trombone, tambourine—and decide for yourself in which groups they belong from the musical groups described.

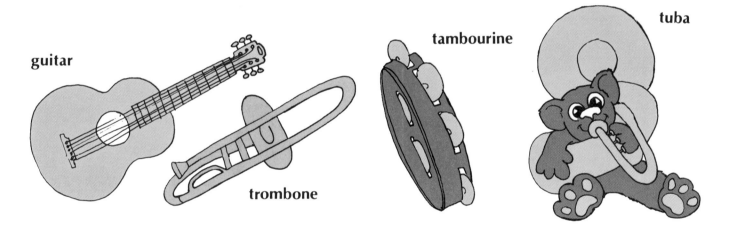

guitar

trombone

tambourine

tuba

Dance to the Music

Dance is more than just movement to music. Like music, it is a language. A *body language,* or how your body talks. Dance expresses ideas and feelings just as music does. It expresses them through the special way feet, hands and head—in fact your whole body—respond to the music.

There are as many dances as there are people. People who make up dances show their own feelings and tell their own stories. Some dances are shared by a large number of people. One group of people is called a *tribe*. A tribe is an extended family of people who started out living together on the same land. To express all the things that are important to the family, a tribe creates a tribal dance. Some countries have national dances — often called folk dances.

Folk dances are part of a people's *tradition*. Tradition is the handing down of beliefs and customs from one generation to the next generation. People do folk dances both for special holidays and just for fun. These dances change slowly over the years. In Asia, for example, some dances are still done the same way as they were 2,000 years ago.

Most folk dances of the United States and Europe are danced by groups in squares (square dances), in circles (rounds), or in two rows facing each other (long-way sets).

Dance and music go hand in hand. The movement in dance matches the rhythm and intensity of the music that goes with it. You could say they grow together. The music of the people of Thailand sounds light, full of tinkling sounds. Thai dance is delicate and bird-like — a perfect match of dance and music. Another example of how music and dance go together is African dance. In African music, many different beats are kept at the same time. In African dance, each part of the body moves — feet, hands and head keep separate beats. African dance looks so lively because it is!

Sometimes a kind of dance becomes popular and millions of people learn it overnight. They dance it in ballrooms, in discos, at parties. These are called dance crazes. Some last, some don't. You probably won't find anyone who knows how to turkey trot anymore. But the twist lives. Ask your parents to show you the twist.

Who Was That?

Sound can play tricks on you. Perhaps you've already been in a cave or near a canyon and been tricked. If not, here's what you'll discover.

Since sound is made up of vibrations or waves in the air, these waves can bounce back at you. If you shout "Hello" across a canyon, a voice comes back saying "Hello." Whatever you shout, the voice repeats exactly. The mystery voice is really your own. What you hear is an *echo*. The sound waves are bouncing off the canyon wall and coming back to your ears. You hear them as an echo.

Behind the Scenes

Bats are small flying animals that live in caves. Bats make good use of echoes. A bat makes sounds that bounce off rocks in the dark caves and other things it might bump into. The echoes tell the bat how far away danger is, so the bat can avoid it.

What You Hear

Sounds are actually *waves* that pass through the air. They stimulate your ear drum and you hear sound. Each sound makes its own unique wave on its way to you.

Each sound wave vibrates at a certain speed. Some waves have 30 vibrations per second. Some have 20,000 vibrations per second. This is called the *frequency* of the sound.

The higher the frequency of a sound, the higher a note sounds. The lower the frequency, the lower a note sounds. This is called *pitch*.

A sound wave can be seen on a special machine. And each wave, of course, looks different.

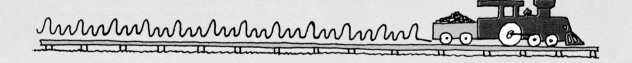

More What You Hear

Here are three waves. Can you guess what sounds they are making?

Sound has two other qualities, *its length and its loudness*. A sound can be long or short. It can be loud or soft. If you listen to all the sounds around you, you can sort them into louder, longer and lower sounds. Or into softer, shorter and higher ones. Like this:

    airplane - low, long, soft
    truck   - low, long, loud
    dog   - high, short, loud
    canary   - high, long, soft

Start your own list.

Behind the Scenes

Words—Wacky and Wise

Language is what we use every day to express our thoughts and feelings. It changes every day. The language that English-speaking people used hundreds of years ago doesn't sound or look like what we use today. Look at the word "sweet." Back then it looked like this: "**Soote**"

The clue to changing language is the people who use it. People use old words in new ways. They shorten or lengthen words. They invent new words for new things. Some of these uses stay in the language. Over a long period of time, speakers of the language may forget how a word started. They just use it. An example is the word Tabasco. Tabasco is a hot sauce named for a river in Mexico. Another is Charleston. The Charleston is a dance that became popular in Charleston, West Virginia. Making up a new word is called "coining" a word. Have you coined any new words lately?

Language can be changed just for fun. Some of these joke languages have remained popular. Pig Latin is one of them. Here's how it works. The first letter or letters before the first vowel of a word are moved to

the end of the word. Then -ay is added. Dog becomes *ogday.* Tree becomes *eetray.* Try it with your own name. (The vowel letters are a, e, i, o and u.)

Another made-up language is Ubbie-dubbie. In Ubbie-dubbie you add -ubb before every vowel in a word. Ubbie-dubbie looks like this. Gubbood nubbight—Good night.

Let's practice these made-up languages. Here are some Pig Latin sentences. Try saying them, then figure out what they mean.

Ancynay otgay otay oolschay atelay isthay orningmay.
Oodgay ightnay!
Oday ouyay atchway eadingray ainbowray?

Now let's practice some Ubbie-dubbie. Once you've mastered these languages, teach a friend—and watch people's faces when they hear you babble away!

Cubban yubbou spubbeak Pubbig Lubbatubbin?
Ubbare cubbats grubbeen?
Mubby Hubballuubowubbeen cubbostubbume wubbas scubbaruuby.

Jungle Life

Jungles and deserts have one thing in common—heat and lots of it. In other ways, they are opposites.

Jungles are located on the *equator.* The equator is an imaginary line that runs around the middle of the earth from east to west. Jungles are also called rain forests because of their heavy yearly rainfall (approximately

60 inches, three times as much as in Los Angeles). Several countries in South America have rain forests. There are also jungles in Africa and elsewhere.

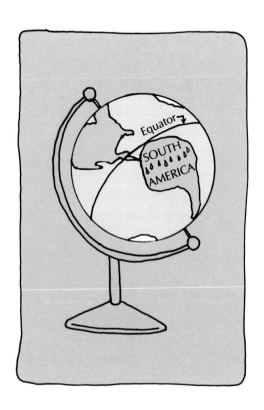

Trees and plants grow very well in these areas because of the heat and *humidity*. Humidity is the amount of moisture in the air.

Food for wildlife is easy to find. All kinds of animals, birds, reptiles and insects thrive in the jungle.

Deserts can be found where yearly rainfall is 10 inches or less. There are five great deserts:

- Arizona/Mexican Sonora Desert
- Sahara Desert in North Africa
- Arabian Desert in Arabian Peninsula
- Gobi Desert in China
- Australian Desert

To learn more about these deserts, look them up in an atlas.

Deserts are the hottest places on earth. Unlike the rain forest, few trees or plants can live in such heat and with so little water. Yet certain plant life has managed to survive. These plants have long roots in order to reach deep down into the earth where water can be found. And they grow thick leaves to hold in the moisture. A cactus is a familiar desert plant.

The animals in the desert can withstand the heat and dryness. Most do not go out during the heat of the day. They only leave their burrows at night. The camel has developed a special water storage area in its stomach, to help it survive in the desert.

Jungle Habitats

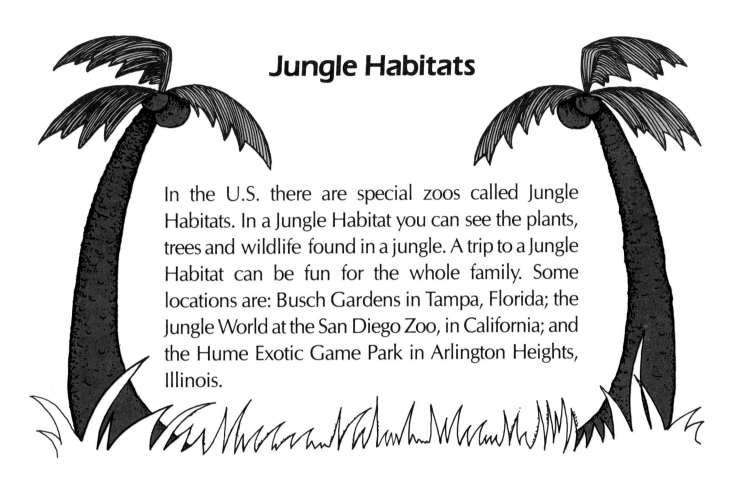

In the U.S. there are special zoos called Jungle Habitats. In a Jungle Habitat you can see the plants, trees and wildlife found in a jungle. A trip to a Jungle Habitat can be fun for the whole family. Some locations are: Busch Gardens in Tampa, Florida; the Jungle World at the San Diego Zoo, in California; and the Hume Exotic Game Park in Arlington Heights, Illinois.

Weather Wise

One reason everyone talks about the weather is that it changes all the time. But how? If you guess wind, you know only one part of the story. There are two more W's in how weather works: warmth and water. Of these, warmth is the most important.

Places at the North Pole and the South Pole do not get much warmth from the sun. Places near the equator get the most. The differences in warmth cause winds to blow between the two places.

Near the equator warm air rises because it is lighter than cool air, and it flows toward the North Pole and the South Pole. Cold air from the poles at the same time is heavier than warm air and travels near the ground. These winds are always switching places with each other.

Water is the third W in the weather picture. That's water as in oceans. The world's oceans help to store up warmth from the sun. In the winter the oceans cool off more slowly than the land. A city near the ocean stays warmer in the winter than a city far away from a coastal area.

Like land, oceans are warmer near the equator and colder near the poles. This difference in water temperatures creates ocean currents. They flow through the water as winds do through the air.

The three W's — warmth, wind and water — mix and match all over the world. Some places have more warmth, some are wetter and some are windier. This combination is called the climate of the place. Can you describe the climate you live in?

A Green Heaven

If you were a plant, you'd choose to live in a jungle. Heat and rainfall are special to all growing things. More kinds of plants grow in a jungle, or rain forest, than anywhere else on earth.

Tropical is another word for the kind of plants that grow in a jungle. Tropical trees usually grow very tall, sometimes more than 160 feet high. They all want to get a fair share of the sunlight. Most of the leaves on these trees are at the top. The tops of the trees make a leafy umbrella over the forest floor.

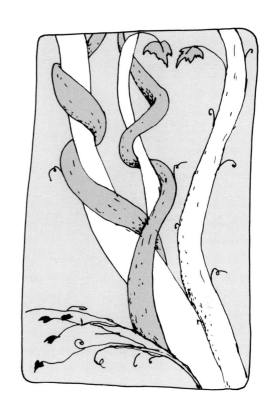

There are many climbing plants in the jungle. They are called *lianas*. These vines climb rocks, trees, and each other, to reach for the sun. Some grow as thick as a man's leg.

The strangest plants in the world are plants that catch insects. Because they eat insects, they are called *carnivorous* (say: car-**niv**-er-us). Carnivorous plants attract insects to their flowers or leaves, trap them, and use the insect as additional food. Although there are over five hundred kinds of carnivorous plants in the world, most of them are found in rain forests or swamps. A popular insect-eating house plant is called a Venus Flytrap, native to North and South Carolina.

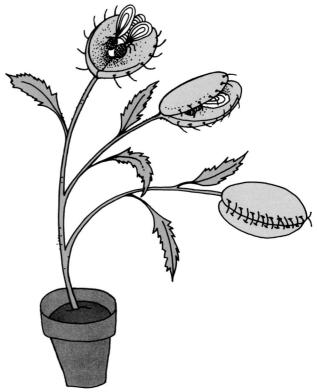

Behind the Scenes

Look Who's Talking!

What would you ask a chimpanzee? Is there a secret you'd like to share with an ape? Don't laugh. Many people talk to apes today.

Although apes do not have the ability to make human voice sounds— they lack a voice box—they are smart enough to learn language. Scientists have taught certain apes sign language. This is the same method of communication used by people who have bad hearing or speech problems.

Experiments with apes have been very successful. Apes not only learn the language but they enjoy using it. One ape made up its own sign for the word "play"—clapping its hands—and only used it when it met a person, another ape, a dog or a cat. Very smart.

The work with apes and language goes on. There's so much to learn. What is language? How do we learn it? How intelligent is the ape compared to people? Someday we'll get the answers to these questions—from an ape.

Computers—What Are They?

Problem solvers? Information keepers? Thought organizers? Computers are all of these things.

If you have an arithmetic problem, a computer can do it faster than you can. And it won't make a mistake. Very difficult problems in mathematics can be done in a flash on a computer. Without one, experts in mathematics would spend days, perhaps weeks, solving the same problem. Computers are very important to science for this reason. The study of science demands a knowledge of math.

You might forget your best friend's telephone number. Or a recipe for fudge. A computer won't. If you tell that telephone number or that recipe to a computer, it will be stored in the computer's memory forever. Or at least until you erase it. That's how well a computer keeps information. The computer translates all information you give it into electrical pulses, or beats. When you ask the computer to recall the information, the storage process works in reverse. It changes information from electrical pulses back into words. Simple? Yes, for a computer.

Behind the Scenes

All the information in a computer—number problems, lists of names and addresses, directions on how to build an airplane—can also be sorted. It can be organized however you need to see it.

How could you use the computer to simplify your life? You could keep a list of all your friends and relatives and their birthdays. You could even instruct the computer to list them by date as well as by name. So you could check, each month, to see who had a birthday coming up. Can you think of other lists and reminders that would help you out?

Where Are They?

The computer is an amazing tool. Many people think it is the most valuable invention of the twentieth century. Computers are important to our daily life in ways we sometimes don't realize.

In medicine there are computers that help doctors find out what's wrong with people.

When you fly in an airplane, your flight is tracked by a computer on the ground. Also, your airline ticket was probably printed by a computer. And the pilot up front learned how to fly the plane by practicing on a computer.

Our government uses computers in many ways. The National Weather Service would be "all wet" all the time if not for the

Reading Rainbow
New York to Denver

Leave 7:17

Arrive 9:50

information gathered and processed by computers. And how else would we get the results of elections so quickly without those trusty computers counting all the votes?

Maybe you've already used a computer at school. There are language courses and math courses that can be taught by a teacher working together with a computer.

How Do They Work?

The computer works very much the way you do to solve a problem. First, you plan the steps you want to follow. The steps for a computer are called a *program*. Then you bring together all your facts and figures. To a computer, this is *input*. You do the organizing and figuring with your brain. The computer does it in its *logic*. At the end you have a solution, or in the language of computers, you have *output*.

Old Is New Again

The way a computer handles information is not new at all. There was a tool invented thousands of years ago in China that worked on math problems in the same way. The tool was called an *abacus* (say: **ab**-uh-kus). The abacus was a wooden frame with wires across it. On each wire there were ten little tiles that filled up part of the wire.

Behind the Scenes

The tiles could then move back and forth. Each tile on the first wire counted as 1. Each tile on the second wire counted as 10. On the third wire each tile counted as 100. When you added or subtracted, you moved the tiles from one side of the frame to the other by 1's, 10's and 100's. For example, if you were adding ten and twelve, you would first move one tile on the second wire (10) and then move another on the second wire (10) plus two on the first wire (1 + 1) to make 12. A quick glance at the moved tiles shows you the answer is 22. You can easily learn to add and subtract on an abacus. It is very much like having a whole group of pairs of hands each with ten fingers!

To learn more about it, why not make an abacus—complete instructions are included in the Activities section of this book.

Computer Talk

Many words in computer talk sound like something you already know. A *menu*, for instance, in computer-ese, doesn't tell you how much a hamburger costs. It is a list of choices at each step of a computer

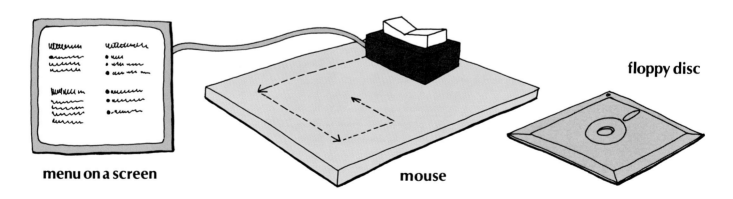

menu on a screen　　　　　　　　　　　**mouse**　　　　**floppy disc**

program. A *floppy* is not a soft, cuddly toy, but a kind of disk. A disk looks like a small phonograph record. You store your computer information on a disk. If a *mouse* is beside your computer, don't worry—it belongs there. In computer talk, a mouse is a small control switch you can hold in your hand.

Robots Today

In science fiction stories, robots were machines that had human shapes. They were created to do work for people, especially dangerous work. Computers today have made robots real. Engineers who design them work in the world of *robotics*.

At first robots were designed for fun. There was one called Squee—for squirrel—that collected golf balls on a golf course. Another, in 1970, was one of the first walking robots. The robot was not a very good walker, as you can tell from its name. It was called Shakey.

Today's robots are dependable. They are an important part of several industries. Car manufacturing is one. Robots spray paint cars and do much of the welding on the assembly line.

51

Activities

One-Kid Band

How many instruments can you play? Are you a one-kid band? With things from around the house you too can become a one-kid band. There may be music hiding in your kitchen. Just take a close look through the cupboards. A cheese grater with a spoon to run across it will make an interesting sound. A whisk broom on a pot sounds whispery and soft. Two pan lids crash like cymbals. Find others to try. Or make these.

1. Put two marbles inside an empty oatmeal box. Tape the lid back on. Shake back and forth.
2. Use an embroidery hoop. Or a yogurt lid with the center punched out. Tie buttons around the edges with string so they dangle and clink against each other.
3. Put dried beans into an empty shoe-polish tin. Shake. If you make two, you can shake one in each hand.

Search For Sounds

Sounds are all around us most of the time. We hear speech, laughter and music. We hear sounds out of doors in the rain—thunder, birds and animals. Day and night we are close to the sound of machines, from alarm clocks and toasters popping to noisy games played at school. But there are sounds around us that we have to look for. Here are two you may have overlooked.

1. Put five glasses on a table. They should all be the same size. Fill each with a different quantity of water. Then gently tap each glass edge with a spoon. Notice the sounds. How do they differ from glass to glass? Glass is a good *conductor* of sound.

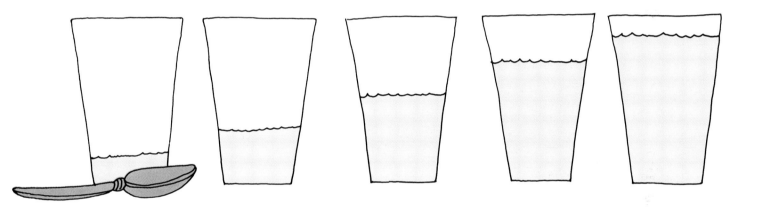

2. Take an empty soda bottle and blow across the top. You will hear a quiet humming sound. The sound changes the harder you blow. How does it change?

Find other sound makers. Tin cans. Paper bags. Look around at home and in your neighborhood and experiment with what you find.

Let's Dance

A *choreographer* is a person who thinks of different movements and arranges them into a whole dance. You can be your own choreographer.

Activities

Think of the dance as a pattern in space. Then listen to several kinds of dance music. What motions do they make you think of? Decide on a favorite song and plan motions to go with the music. They can be hops, sways, jumps, skips, slides, runs or bends. Use your arms too. Practice until you know your dance well. Then show it off!

Trivia Game

Trivia are facts that may be unimportant but are very interesting. You can make up a game using trivia. Here are some to start you off. Put them on cards. Write the question on one side and the answer on the other. Stump your friends.

1. Q. Which is colder, the Arctic (North Pole) or the Antarctic (South Pole)?
   A. The Antarctic is because the land is high and mountainous.
2. Q. What animal tells you the temperature?
   A. A cricket. Count the number of chirps in a minute, divide the total by four, then add forty to find out how hot it is.
3. Q. How do trees tell you it's going to rain?
   A. Their leaves curl under. Check it out next time a storm is on the way.

Count On It

For thousands of years arithmetic was done on an abacus. Follow these simple steps to make your own.

1. Find a gift box or shoe box.

2. Cut out the bottom.

3. Put three holes on one side like this.

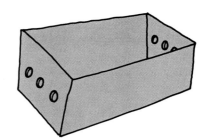

4. Put three more holes on the opposite side. The three pairs of holes should be across from each other.

5. Find 30 buttons and three long pieces of yarn.

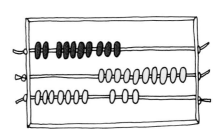

6. String 10 buttons on each piece of yarn.

7. Put one end of the yarn through the first hole and knot it on the outside of the box. Then put the other end through the opposite hole, pull the yarn tight, and knot it on the outside. It should look like this.

8. Repeat with the next two pieces of yarn.

You can add up to 1,110 on your abacus. You can count on it!

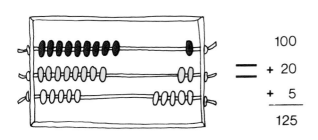

$$
\begin{array}{r}
100 \\
+\ 20 \\
+\ \ 5 \\
\hline
125
\end{array}
$$

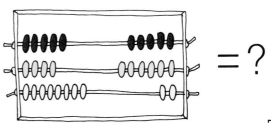

$= ?$

55

Activities

A Field Guide To Your Neighborhood

You don't have to live in a jungle to be surrounded by fascinating trees. Wherever you live, there's a variety of them. Learn about the trees in your neighborhood. How tall will they grow? Where else do they grow? Are the trees used for wood, for paper, for food (like the maple tree that gives us maple syrup)?

Make a guide to the trees around you. This kind of guide is called a field guide. Here's how to get started.

1. Collect leaves from your neighborhood—each a different kind, of course.
2. Go to the library for a book on trees and their leaves.
3. Compare your leaves to the drawings or photographs in the book. Name the tree each leaf comes from and read about it.
4. Press each leaf in a piece of clear plastic wrap and tape each into a notebook.
5. Write down the information you've learned about each tree next to the leaf.

CHESTNUT OAK
Grows straight, tall.
Many kinds. all grow acorns.
Leaf: sharp pointed ends and lobes
   shaped like triangles. In fall
   leaves turn red.
Found all over U S.
Leaf found: school yard.
Date: March 18. 1986.

WHITE SPRUCE
Height: 40-90 feet.
Trunk: 1-2 feet thick.
Branches sweep down, turn up at end.
Needles: less than 1" long with
    blue-green color.
Used to make paper.
Northern and Northwest U.S.
Leaf found: Back yard.
Date: January 1. 1986.

BLACK LOCUST
Height: 80 feet average.
Trunk: 1-3 feet thick.
Leaves are pretty, blossoms are white.
Leaves yellow-green; at night and
    when it rains, leaves close up.
Wood good for fuel.
Found in Southern U.S. forests.
Leaf found: On trip through Texas.
Date: September 3. 1986

How To Do A Folk Dance

Most folk dances have easy steps. That way
everyone can join in. Here's one for you to
learn. It's from Scotland, and it's called the
Highland Fling.

Activities

1. Hop on your left foot, touch your right toe to the side of your left leg.
2. Hop on your left foot, raise your right foot in front of your left knee, bending right knee and pointing your toe to the ground.
3. Hop on your right foot, touch your left toe to the side of your right leg.
4. Hop on your right foot, raise your left foot in front of your right knee, bending left knee and pointing your toe to the ground.
5. Repeat with your arms curved over your head.

When the music bounces, so will you when you're doing the Fling. Teach it to a friend, and you can dance together.

Now Hear This!

Words that sound like what they mean are called *onomatopeia*. (say: ah-no-mah-tah-**pee**-uh). *Splat*, for example. Or *gooey*. You probably stumble across them everywhere — even at the dinner table. Here are four sentences with the onomatopeia missing. Match up the right word with right sound in each sentence.

crunch   1. Mom told my brother not to _____ his soup.
slurp   2. When the fork hits my teeth, I hear a _____.
gulp   3. Raw carrots _____ when you eat them.
clink   4. You shouldn't _____ your milk.

Jokes

Q: Why don't more elephants water ski?
A: Very few own boats.

A boy was told to take care of his little sister while his parents were away. He decided to go fishing and took her along.

"I'll never do that again," the boy told his mother later. "I didn't catch a thing."

Mother said, "I'm sure she'll be quiet next time if you just explain to her that fish run away when there's noise."

"It wasn't the noise," the boy said. "She ate the bait."

Sammy had just finished his first day of school.

"What did you learn today?" asked his mother.

"Not enough, I have to go back tomorrow."

Activities

Hide And Seek

Every person on this bus paid bus fare to the driver. But there are three robots on the bus, too, and they didn't pay their fares. The bus driver is looking for them. Can you help find them?

Did You Know...?

- If there was a road around the earth at the equator, you would have to walk 23 miles a day for 23 years to circle the earth.

- The Sahara, the world's largest desert, is as large as all of Europe.

- Three-quarters of the world's fresh water is in *glaciers*. Glaciers are the great rivers of ice that cover the poles and the earth's high mountains.

Word Search

Hidden in the maze below are words you've just learned. Do you remember what they mean? The words go across and down. Find the words in the maze, then write them on another paper.

EQUATOR, WEATHER, JUNGLE, DANCE, COMPUTER, DISK, MOUSE, ROBOT, INPUT, OUTPUT, TROPICAL, LIANA, WAVE

D	I	S	K	N	W	A	V	E	E
A	W	N	D	I	E	Z	T	L	Q
N	B	B	I	N	A	R	Y	P	U
C	O	M	P	U	T	E	R	N	A
E	U	O	K	C	H	V	O	E	T
C	T	U	R	H	E	W	B	L	O
F	P	S	S	U	R	K	O	I	R
J	U	E	I	N	P	U	T	A	L
M	T	J	U	N	G	L	E	N	X
O	Q	T	R	O	P	I	C	A	L

Activities

Behind The Scenes

Sound can be imitated because some sounds are very familiar. We do not have to see the source of the sound to know what it is. In movies, on television or on stage, a sound is often imitated. This is called a *sound effect*. Here are some of them you can try at home.

Fire   A piece of clear, stiff cellophane, crinkled gently, sounds like bacon and eggs frying. Crumpling it more vigorously changes the sound to a raging fire. Close your eyes and use your imagination.

Horse   1.   Hold two paper cups, one in each hand, and bring the open ends together.
2.   Swing one hand up as the other goes down.
3.   Brush the open ends of the cups past each other. It sounds like a horse trotting. Doing the up-down-touch motion faster makes the horse gallop.

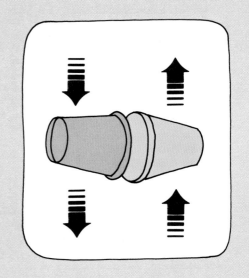

Grow A Tree

Grow a little avocado tree. It grows very quickly, and you can enjoy watching how the plant changes from week to week. All you need is an avocado pit, a plastic cup at least 5" high, four toothpicks, a pot (8"-10" across), and some potting soil. Follow these simple steps.

1. Put four toothpicks into the avocado pit like this.
2. Put the pit in a glass of water (pointy side up). The toothpicks should hold at least half the pit out of the water.
3. Place the glass in a warm spot but not in the sun. The kitchen is a good place to keep it. Add water occasionally.
4. Soon you will see roots begin to form. Watch the changes as the pit splits and the first green shoot comes out at the top of the pit.
5. Remove the toothpicks and transfer the roots and pit gently to the pot. Soil should cover only half the pit. Water your growing plant once a week.

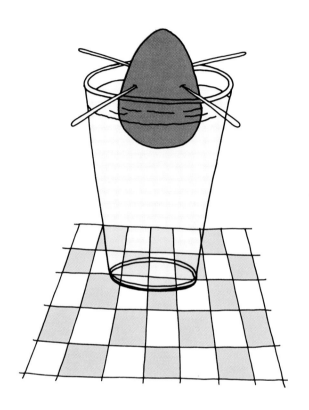

A Clown Trick

The clowns in this picture are playing tricks on you. Find what's changing in each picture.

Activities

Be Your Own Weather Station

A weather forecaster has to study *meteorology* (pronounce every syllable). Meteorology is the science of how weather works. The forecaster has to understand how weather patterns form, how they move around the world, and how these different weather patterns react to each other when they meet.

You can study your local weather. To set up your own weather station, use these simple tools you can make yourself.

- If you tie a piece of yarn to a Popsicle stick and hold it up high, you can see which way the wind is blowing.
- Mark the side of a paper cup with a ruler at ¼″ and ½″ and ¾″ and 1″. Set it out when it rains. After the storm, see how much rain fell.